Book 2

UNDER NAZI RULE

The Dutch in Wartime
Survivors Remember

Edited by

Tom Bijvoet

Mokeham Publishing Inc.

© 2011, 2014 Mokeham Publishing Inc.
P.O. Box 35026, Oakville, Ontario, L6L 0C8, Canada
P.O. Box 559, Niagara Falls, New York, 14304, USA
www.mokeham.com

Cover photograph courtesy of Gemeente Gorinchem

ISBN 978-0-9868308-3-9

Contents

Introduction

Tom Bijvoet

Growing up in The Netherlands in the 1960s and 1970s I must have heard the words "Well, it's clear that you did not experience the war!", accurate and true as they are, hundreds, maybe even thousands of times. As an educational multi-purpose tool, probably quite out of keeping with the advice of good Dr. Spock, a whole generation of Dutch children was subjected to this useful mantra. Sadness about a broken toy: "well, during the war we had no toys, they were all traded for food". Homesick during a sleepover with relatives: "well, during the war I spent seven months away from my family with total strangers." And the word 'hungry' was taboo for many people: "You are not hungry, you only have a mild appetite, in the war we were hungry."

When I was a young child, every adult over about twenty-five years of age had experienced the German occupation. Parents, teachers, aunts, uncles, pastors, soccer coaches, the milkman, the baker and the greengrocer: "Well, in the war ...".

As I edited this second volume of memories of survivors of the Nazi-German occupation of The Netherlands in World War II, it struck me how all-encompassing the impact of the occupation was on everyone, every day in almost every ordinary activity. What we take for granted, everything we do without thinking about it, became a chore or a burden during the war. Schooling was interrupted, because Germans converted entire buildings into barracks. Putting food on the table required long waits in line-ups, careful planning to ensure meager rations would last and continuous bartering and hustling to supplement those meager rations. There was not one aspect of life, from clothing the family and doing the laundry to visiting friends at night and keeping the house lit and warm, that was not difficult. Daily survival required forethought, planning and extra effort. But even with the extra effort failure, frustration and real hardship were common. And we're only talking about daily life here. Add to the challenges of going about one's business the danger inherent in the wartime situation such as bombing raids and the random reprisals by the Germans, who often victimized innocent civilians as a punishment for acts of resistance.

The difficulty in running one's life was often exacerbated by the requirement to take people in, strangers often, for months or years on end: families who had been bombed out of their houses, people who had been evacuated from areas where the Germans did not want them, young men on the run for the dreaded obligation to perform forced labor in Germany and children who had been sent to the country by their city-dwelling parents to ensure that they got a slightly better diet. And then of course there were the resistance workers and Jews hiding from the Germans. Putting up those required real courage, nerves of steel and the willingness to risk one's own life. Or at the other end of the spectrum and almost as threatening one could be forced to billet German soldiers.

In this second volume of the 'Dutch in Wartime' series of books we have collected a number of recollections related to everyday survival during the German occupation of The Netherlands. We get a glimpse of the terror that was inherent in the occupation, but in this book we are predominantly confronted with the struggle for every day survival during the first years of the war, before things got really bad, as we can say now, in hindsight and with astonishment. As we read these memories we wonder how things could have gotten worse, but they did. We marvel at the capacity of human beings to absorb hardship, setbacks, substandard living conditions and fear – and still help others. It is no wonder that as kids we heard so much about the war. That was all there was, for five long years: one big struggle for survival, even when it came to the most mundane of activities. And that struggle passed no one by, just like it passes no one by who lives in a war torn part of the world today. Because let us not forget the devastating fact that similar memories are being created today. I would like to thank all contributors to this volume for sharing their stories with us, maybe they will help by way of warning to prevent at least some similar memories from forming in the future.

Historical background

Hostilities in The Netherlands at the start of World War II lasted five days, from May 10, 1940, when the German army invaded the country, until May 14, when the city center of Rotterdam was destroyed in a devastating bombing attack. A fleet of Heinkel bombers carpet-bombed the city, 800 Rotterdammers lost their lives and 80,000 lost their homes. Utrecht would receive the same treatment, the Germans warned, and so on down the list, city after city, until the Dutch surrendered. On May 15 General Winkelman, the Dutch commander in chief, signed the armistice treaty. German forces swarmed into The Netherlands and occupied the country.

The Germans installed a civilian, rather than a military regime in The Netherlands. The idea was to win the support of their Germanic Dutch 'cousins' for National Socialism.

Therefore the occupation started off relatively mildly and the Germans did not seem that bad after all. The population engaged in some moderate demonstrations of opposition to the occupying authorities, particularly focused on showing their ongoing support for the exiled House of Orange. The Germans clamped down on these and very soon came to the conclusion that they would not win the support of the Dutch people, with the exception of a very small minority of fanatical National Socialists supplemented by some unscrupulous opportunists, who saw a chance to profit from the war.

Some insightful people had never bought in to the soft approach that the Germans had initially taken and the first underground resistance groups had been formed as early as May 15, 1940. The major turning point however, was the 1941 'February Strike' in Amsterdam. As a protest against the first big round-up of Jews in Amsterdam, which was accompanied by severe violence, transit and other municipal workers walked off the job. The strike quickly spread to the private sector and within a few hours was close to universal. The strike spread to surrounding cities and towns like Haarlem, Zaandam and Hilversum. The Germans punished the strikers with severe measures, revealing their true nature and intentions.

The grip on the population became harsher. Artists, doctors and other professionals were forced to join German-led 'guilds' if they wanted to continue practicing their trades. Many refused and went into hiding. Students were forced to sign a 'declaration of loyalty' to the occupying authorities. Many refused and went into hiding. Those who were caught were either sent to Germany to work on farms and in factories or were sent to prison.

On a gradual basis ever larger groups of men and boys were required to go to work in Germany. Many refused and went into hiding.

People were issued with identity cards that everyone had to carry on their person at all times. German military or police could demand to see those whenever they wanted to. Checkpoints were set up at roadsides, in railway stations and checks took place on trains, in streetcars, at sporting events, outside theaters, anywhere where people who did not comply with the edicts of the authorities could be caught.

Curfews were implemented forbidding people from

being outside at night.

The Germans controlled information and communications. Listening to radio broadcasts from London was forbidden and everybody was forced to hand in their radios. Many hid theirs and listened secretly at significant risk to themselves and their families. Underground groups published and distributed newsletters and newspapers, with potential life-threatening consequences for the organizers.

Rationing of food, clothing and essential household items started to weigh heavily on the Dutch people. The rationing system itself was quite complicated and often people had to stand in line for long times to even get the articles they were entitled to under the rationing system.

Another side effect of the rationing system was that it made it much harder to go into hiding. Being underground meant not getting ration cards. No ration cards: no food, no soap, no shoes, no clothes. A huge underground industry in forging both identity cards and ration cards for those in hiding, or active in the Resistance, developed.

Resistance groups were chased down fanatically and when caught their members would be cruelly tortured and summarily executed. Traitors and careless talk could literally kill a person. The Germans were not beyond taking hostages and executing innocent civilians in response to actions by the Resistance.

Plunder started. Bicycles, food, industrial equipment, everything was shipped off to Germany. And eventually the Germans started to round up all the able-bodied men they could get their hands on to send them to Germany.

Survival itself had become a struggle for the vast majority of the Dutch population.

War! War!

John Eyking

My father was a market gardener in Beverwijk and he was cutting spinach at 5 a.m. on May 10, 1940 when he ran into our house, waking the family by hollering "war, war!". He had seen the parachutes dropping down in our neighborhood. We all gathered in front of our small black radio and listened to announcements and warnings about how to deal with strangers. One way we were told to check on them was to ask them to pronounce 'Scheveningen'. Apparently only a Dutch person can pronounce that name correctly. At school that morning the Principal sent us home. For the rest of the war, we only went to school for half a day sharing the time with students from another school, because our school had been turned into a German barracks.

The occupation troops demanded that the population turn over amongst other items their radios, bikes, horses and blankets. Everything we produced was recorded. Sketches were made of cows and fields. If your cow did not produce any offspring, the local vet had to give you a statement confirming that. The crops on the fields were recorded and you were told what part of your harvest was to be given to the occupying forces. We grew tulip, daffodil and hyacinth bulbs. Since there was no possibility to export those we kept a small amount of foundation seed so we would be ready after the war and instead of bulbs, we began to grow vegetables, grains and fruits.

Later came the bombing of the steel plant that was directly across from our farm and the submarine port in IJmuiden. Thousands of planes from England would fly directly over our farm daily on their way to bomb northern Germany. Two hours later they could be seen returning from their missions. Many were shot down over us. Food became scarcer by the day. Food coupons were used for every food item and the rations became smaller all the time. Bread was made from a mixture of potatoes, tulip bulbs and some grain.

The Germans held round-ups to catch men who refused to work in Germany. Beverwijk was surrounded and closed off from the outside world during one of these round-ups and almost 500 residents were picked up and sent to work camps in Germany. More than 60 of these people did not return.

Before the war we had a thriving Jewish community in Beverwijk with its own Synagogue. Unfortunately, no more than 30 members of this community survived the war.

I never saw them again

Roland Krijgsman

After the Dutch army capitulated more German soldiers came to our island of Goeree-Overflakkee, where I lived in the town of Middelharnis as a twelve year old. They brought anti-aircraft guns and some pieces of artillery. They commandeered a number of houses and some of the farmers were forced to transport food for the troops.

In the evening hours English planes flew over and German flak fired at them. They also used a huge searchlight to catch the English planes in a beam of light. Cars were commandeered too and a number of men were ordered to make two of the local schools ready to house German soldiers including the dreaded SS.

Every week the German troops held exercises in the polders and in our little harbor.

We were not allowed to fly the Dutch flag anymore, but one of the village grocery stores displayed the Dutch tricolor on the Queen's birthday. A week later the store was bombed and three people lost their lives. The bomb had been dropped by a German plane.

In wintertime a storm blew the electric cables of the German command post against a streetcar and the lines broke. Thinking this was an act of sabotage, fifteen men were randomly selected and sent to the prison camp in Schoorl for four months of hard labor.

Above Herkingen, a village about four miles from Middelharnis, an English bomber was shot down. Only one member of the four-man crew survived.

In the evenings we sat by the window and watched the searchlights. We could hear the grenades exploding. A night-time curfew was also implemented.

Some girls kept the German soldiers company, so you had to be careful about what you said. Food was getting scarce and we got ration coupons for many items. The ferry was shot at by English Spitfires and ever more men were forced to work for the Germans, many of them were sent to Germany.

A few months after Pearl Harbor we saw the first American bombers fly over. The Germans brought more anti-aircraft guns to our island. We had to hand in all our copper and tin. The church bells were taken from the steeples. Many cows and horses were also taken by the Germans.

In 1942 the approximately 45 Jewish families were deported to concentration camps in Germany and Poland. Not one person returned. I had Jewish friends, the Mezrits, Slager, Hagen and Polak families. I never saw them again.

Evacuated and put to work

John Inthout

I was nine years old when my mother called us outside to show us the red sky over Rotterdam after it had been bombed. It was clearly visible from Scheveningen, where we lived and I remember that sight to this day. My mother was a widow with two children, my seven year old brother and me. We were forced to leave our house, because it was too close to the coast, where the Germans wanted to build fortifications.

We were evacuated to a small town called Maurik, near Tiel. I was not allowed to stay with my mother. I was placed with a milkman and my mother and brother ended up with a farmer who was married, but did not have any children. It was difficult to adapt to the new surroundings. I remember that they spoke a dialect there that was hard for me to understand. One day the milkman asked me to get a jug of cream from the cellar. I went downstairs and saw what I recognized as cream. I filled a jug and went back upstairs, but apparently I had done something wrong, I should have brought up a jug of milk. In their dialect the word for milk sounded like our word for cream. At least I was never sent down to the cellar again.

The Germans told the people who were forced to take us in that it was only for three months, after which we would be moved to other families. After three months my mother and brother were moved to another family, the village blacksmith, who was also married without children. I was moved from the milkman to the miller, who had three daughters, but no sons. One of the daughters dated the baker, who figured he could use me in the bakery. He had trouble getting out of bed, so the wheat salesman had me throw little rocks up against his bedroom window to wake him up. When he was awake he let me in and then we would start making bread. First we would have to light the fire in the oven with twigs and branches. I learnt the whole process of baking bread. Then when the bread was ready at about nine a.m. we would put big baskets on our bicycles and start delivering the bread to our clients. It took a little while to learn to manipulate a bike with a huge breadbasket on the front.

It was about a five mile ride to the most distant client, a farmer. His farm was at least a ten minute bike ride from the main highway across an unpaved cart path. When it had rained it was very slippery and it was difficult to keep the heavy bike upright with my short legs. They took ten large loaves there, but that did not lighten your load, because the farmer's wife would give you ten bags of flour in return to bake the next lot of bread.

Always something exciting going on

Frans Dullemond

The first war years were rather uneventful for me as a young boy living in Apeldoorn. That changed in a hurry when my dad's company asked him to move to the small town of Neede in the East of the country to set up a knife factory. From the day of the move, there was always something exciting going on.

There was a plant there where the Germans used to store their stolen goods: radios, cars and many other items. The allies bombed the plant and the Germans sprung into action. They removed all the stolen vehicles and parked them along the road to the railway station. Most of them were pretty old. For us as young boys all that was very interesting. We would sneak into these cars and play with them. There was a guard at the railway station, but he did not pay attention to playing children. One car was very interesting, because it seemed to have a different kind of propulsion. It was parked with its nose against a large storage shed, where coal was stored when it was still available. We turned the ignition key. There was no sound, so I put my foot on the accelerator and immediately the vehicle moved so fast that it created a big hole in the side of the shed. That made a lot of noise, so the German guard was alerted and he moved much quicker than we had ever thought possible. But we were just as quick. We jumped out and ran away as fast as we could.

The guard followed us for a bit. I was expecting him to shoot, but he did not. During our hasty escape I jumped over a low wire fence, tripped and hurt my shinbone. A small wound was the result.

We kept running until we were out of sight of the station and hid for a while. Apparently we had come across a vehicle with electric propulsion and a battery that was still very much alive.

The small wound on my shin soon became infected and it turned into a big sore. I had more of those sores, and they just did not heal. After months I was sent to our family doctor. He cleaned my sores and gave me some kind of ointment to put on it daily. It did not seem to work and I went back to him several times until he decided to put just adhesive tape on the sores and told me to leave it on. I had to come back a week later. My mother was hopping mad about that approach but there was improvement now. The treatment was repeated and soon the sores started to become smaller and smaller until they finally disappeared. I had those sores for more than a year. I have a big scar on my shin to this day.

It was this same plant, where all the stolen stuff was stored, that was the target for nightly excursions by the local population to steal back the occasional item. Of course there were guards on duty but that did not seem to deter anybody. My dad went on such an excursion and came home with dynamos and headlights for a bicycle and also radio cabinets which were used by me as a closet to stow my toys.

All during the war the Germans enforced a curfew. When something had to be organized that should not be noticed by the Germans darkness was a good cover but also risky. The Germans patrolled the streets. Getting heating fuel was difficult especially since it was forbidden to fell trees for that purpose. There were enough trees around because there were some forests nearby. So it was really tempting to cut down trees. The difficulty was that doing it in daytime was too obvious and one could be caught quickly. Doing it at night was rather difficult, because of the curfew.

My father and his brother Jan planned to do something. So they left quietly when no German patrol was in sight. Behind our backyard ran an old railroad track which was rarely used. They followed the track knowing that few Germans would go there. They had a cart to haul the logs home. A few kilometers down they felled a tree and hauled it back to our backyard where they cut it to pieces over the next few days, completely undetected by the Germans. It kept us all warm for a little while. Now that there was fuel, we needed kindling to light a fire in the furnace. I was given that task, so every day I had to make kindling of old wood and twigs and smaller branches.

By the last year of the war there was hardly anything available in the stores. Clothes for us children were made from our parents' old clothes. Shoes were not available at all, so when shoes became too small, the noses and or heels were cut out. To some extent we were lucky that wooden shoes could still be obtained, albeit at a high price.

Wooden shoes when new are not very comfortable. They became more comfortable when they started to wear down. I wore linings in them which were either made from soft leather or knitted wool. Of course I did everything in them, walking, running, playing soccer. These wooden shoes wore down and weakened easily and sooner or later they would break, either during a game of soccer or while running. Whenever those things broke I was afraid to go home, because of mother's anger that would invariably ensue. She would deliver a tirade designed to make me feel guilty, not only about those wooden shoes, but also about how difficult a life she had. Then usually she later complained to my dad and he added insult to injury. It never resulted in getting new wooden shoes, they were usually repaired. An iron band around the shoe would make it seem whole again and by the time the soles became too thin dad would cover them with old pieces of leather which he got from the factory. They were used there to hone razorblades and when they had worn too small they were discarded and of course my dad saw a good application in attaching them to the soles of shoes and wooden shoes. The very first time that I remember getting new clothes was in 1948, three years after the war, when I was 12 years old.

My dad was often sent on strange and sometimes dangerous missions. A knife factory truck had gone to Hengelo and had broken down at a plant where they produced electric motors. The wood-gas generator of the truck had broken which had rendered the vehicle useless. So dad towed a welding machine and some tools on a cart behind his bike over a distance of about 25 miles. He arrived at his destination and started repairing the truck. In the meantime, however, the Germans had started a raid to round-up workers to be sent to Germany as slave laborers. He was not aware of that and ended up in a line of captured men, despite showing the pass that exempted him from call-up. By talking to a sympathetic officer he managed to get himself and the truck driver out.

One of the very nice things of Neede and the region called the 'Achterhoek' was that there was a tradition called 'nabuurplicht' (neighbor duty). The idea is to help each other out if someone nearby is in trouble. All one needed to do is ask, or sometimes even that was not necessary. One of our neighbors was a widow and she had a big yard where she grew vegetables and potatoes and also kept a couple of pigs. Each year in the late fall some of these were slaughtered. Then she was busy for several days preparing sausages and cutting and smoking the meat and bacon. She would always bring our family some sausages and bacon, especially in the period when nothing could be bought, because the butcher could not get anything anymore.

Another neighbor was the mayor during the occupation, they appointed him because he was a collaborator. During the latter part of the war there were several air raids and to protect the neighbors he let us shelter in his concrete reinforced cellar. We spent several hours there being scared and listening to explosions.

Not all Germans were repulsive, some were nice. Across from our house was a car maintenance workshop and the Germans had commandeered it and used it for repairs. As children we went there out of curiosity. Cleaning ourselves was a major chore because soap was not available. One of the Germans must have noticed how dirty we were when we went there. He went inside and gave my sister a huge bar of toilet soap. That was really a treasure. But we hated their patrols in the street. They walked in pairs along our street. They were armed heavily and had a rifle with bayonet in place and a bag full of ammunition and two big hand grenades stuck between their belts. In the evening they watched for any trace of light coming from windows and they would knock on those doors where they had seen something.

Giving birth
during an air raid

Trix Barlage Bodde

My mother Janny wrote down the following story about my birth on April 1, 1943: At the start of the war papa and I had known each other for five years, but for financial reasons we were not yet married. We had already bought many pieces of furniture and my trousseau was complete. We lived in Rotterdam and we finally found a beautiful upstairs apartment to rent near the bombed-out area and got married in 1941. The first few years of the war were not bad. We did have curfews, but we went to see people, had guests, and played bridge. I took courses in baby and child care, learned how to make toys out of old newspapers and whatnot. We were issued proof of identification and food coupons.

In August of 1942 I became pregnant. We furnished your room just like a picture in a magazine. I was sure you would be a girl, I did not want a boy who would be drafted.

March 31, 1943: Bright blue skies. I am extremely tired. Have been in bed for a month already, doctor's orders. Droning in the distance, dozens of black dots in the sky, very high. British planes on the way to Germany. Suddenly, air raid! Bombs all around us. Are they crazy? They are much too high to hit any target. They try to bomb the Merwe Harbor, but because they want to stay out of reach of the anti-aircraft guns, the bombs fall on the Rotterdam Dike and on the houses, which we overlook from our apartment. Better get dressed.

We have to leave. But how? Trams are flat on the street. Utter chaos. No way! I cannot walk in this condition. Finally the all-clear. Papa's friend Henk at the door. Says we cannot stay and we should come with him. There is a train to Schiedam from Central Station. Pack the flight suitcase, we'll go to the station in Schiedam and we'll see if we can get to the suburb of Hillegersberg where papa's parents live. On our way: two men and I with a very big belly. My subconscious notices a sign: Boerhave Clinic, private maternity hospital. Arriving at the station we realize that hundreds of people had the same idea. Suddenly I feel something warm and wet on my leg. My waters have broken. So we turn around and go to the clinic. The two men go on to Hillegersberg. I stay behind in a cold clinic filled with Jewish girls in hiding and two mothers with babies. We still hear roaring in the skies. The nurse tells me to keep walking until I really cannot stay on my feet and am taken to a delivery room, a high white cold space with windows covered with black paper. The nurses disappear from time to time because the air raids come and go. Between two air raids the nurse decides to look in, and suddenly I have the most beautiful baby in the whole world, a month premature.

It is April 1 now and papa still does not know. Telephones do not work. The next day brings a proud father. He must register the girl in Schiedam. Beatrix? No sir, not allowed, the oldest grandchild of the queen is called Beatrix. Royal names are forbidden by the Germans. During my three weeks in the clinic papa dismantles the apartment, which is undamaged, and gives notice. We are going to his parents in Hillegersberg. They all mean well but it is a big blow for me.

A hospital makes way for the Atlantic Wall

Carla de Boer

My parents moved with me to a part of The Hague called the 'Vogelwijk' in 1926. I was just over one year old at the time. The house overlooked the Red Cross Hospital. After a couple of years I was able to see the hospital from the guestroom on the third floor if I stood on a footstool. Next door to us lived a family with three daughters. The middle one wanted to become a doctor and I wanted to become a nurse. There were many kids on our block. We played outside after supper, all the kids would ride tricycles, scooters, you name it. At seven p.m. the parents would pick up their kids and take them home. One of our favorite games was playing 'hospital'.

In the evening my parents loved to go for a stroll and I went along. Reaching Sport Avenue we could see the lights of the hospital. Bright lights were on in the operating rooms. We would say: they are busy again. I thought they were performing surgery, but when I started training to be a nurse in 1945 I learned that it was nurses setting up the tables for the next day.

In 1942 the Nazis ordered management to evacuate the whole hospital and to leave by a certain date. That was insane of course but the Germans thought that if they fortified the coast the allied troops would not be able to land. It also meant that on one side of Sport Avenue a whole row of houses would be flattened. They spared the beautiful houses just behind the sand dunes. German troops occupied those. They kept all utilities working in this neighborhood. My Mom was very ill and my Dad managed to have us stay in our house for an extra year. It was like living in a ghost town. I would roam around and look for something to eat in the gardens of the empty houses. I brought home apples and pears and berries and for my mom I found plenty of flowers to cheer her up. I also noticed that the Germans were removing all copper door handles, hinges and bathtubs from the abandoned houses. So my dad and I started to do that too in our house, but we went into the crawl space and buried everything we could.

The hospital was to be relocated to a building that was a retirement home. To make space for the hospital all the old people were sent further inland, to areas like Gelderland. Next door to the building were tiny houses around little courtyards. The staff found places to live there. It all belonged to the Dutch Reformed Church.

The patients were sent home or to the South Shore Hospital. Everybody who worked in the hospital, doctors, nurses, cooks, became demolition workers. After all the beds were sent to the new location the next round started, with pots and pans, furnaces, faucets, electrical wiring, pipes and other reusable materials. When a ward was empty they would celebrate with a couple of games of soccer.

There were not enough toilets and bathtubs in the new building so the materials from the old building came in handy. There was of course a shortage of trucks and drivers. Many working age men had gone into hiding. The doctors also had to go into hiding, especially when there was a raid. There was room in a crawlspace under the first aid clinic.

Not everything fit into the new place. The University Hospital in Leiden made room for the overstock which was saved until after the war was over. The enormous autoclaves and the basin in which trays and instruments for surgery had to be boiled also had to be moved to the new location. A huge bin with coal to start the little potbelly stoves was another big item that made the trip across town.

During all the bleakness there was also sometimes time for some fun. One day during a break the head nurse came with coffee. One of the doctors sat down on a toilet seat and said: "well Sister, why don't you come and sit next to me. I would never have thought that I would sit together with you on the toilet!"

Nurses crawled between floors to remove electric wiring. On the last day there was only one functional toilet left. It was not flushed so that the Germans would find a 'gift' to welcome them.

In the new place there was only one toilet for about thirty patients. In a little room next to the wards were a couple of sinks. A shelf was put on top of the sinks and this became the spot to make sandwiches. Towards the end of the war it became impossible to heat the whole hospital. One hot water bottle went from one bed to the next. There was a living room with clotheslines where all the hospital linen was hung to dry. During the night the nurses were back to the days of Florence Nightingale, using candles and lanterns. Left-over wax from the candles was used over and over. Bed sheets were changed every two weeks if not too soiled. The same with towels, one for the top and one for the bottom. Everybody survived and strangely enough I did not see as many infections as we have in hospitals now.

We walked into a small building

Toni Trommelen

I lived in Rotterdam during the war, I was 13 when it started and 18 when it ended. I did not do anything heroic but maybe this is news for some people. All the libraries were closed during the war, but our church made its own library. We were not allowed to go ballroom dancing, only folk dancing was allowed. So they had folk dances every Sunday. Halfway through the war all the boys were taken to Germany or went into hiding. So we went on with only girls dancing.

During the war we had to close every window with black paper so no light would shine outside. We were not allowed to be outside in the evening. One evening I went to my girlfriend's and my father picked me up. We were walking in the middle of the street. There was no moon and it was so dark we walked straight into a small building, we could not see it, it was pitch-black.

Life in the Frisian countryside

John Keulen

During the early years of German occupation life went on fairly normally in my home town of Bakhuizen, just inland from Stavoren. Six Germans serving as occupation troops were stationed in Mirns, a neighboring hamlet. Their commanding officer Hans (an Austrian) stayed there for most of the war. The rest of the men were on rotation from the front and their duties were considered R and R (Rest and Recuperation). These battle-hardened soldiers were glad to get in some leisure time and were usually cordial and friendly to the local populace. Some of these soldiers came from the Russian Front and father talked to one who had actually seen the spires of Moscow through his binoculars before his unit was forced to retreat to prevent encirclement by a Russian counter attack.

Hans got to know many of the merchants and storekeepers in town, and even befriended my father, a fact which would prove beneficial later in the war. Subtle changes were in the offing however. The three cafés were required to hang signs in their windows reading 'No Jews allowed'. Jews were also required to wear a large yellow star of David when outside. As there were no Jews in Bakhuizen, and the town was rarely visited by Jews, these orders did not mean much to us.

More noticeable changes were the introduction of ration cards for food staples like bread, butter, sugar, meat, and many other products. These were very important to people living in the big cities who had little opportunity to obtain clandestine food in the country. In our small rural village many people grew their own potatoes and vegetables, kept a few animals, or were able to buy milk at local dairy farms.

The Germans forced farmers to grow quotas of various grains according to acreage. The harvest was destined for Germany and the war effort. They enforced ever more rules like curfews at night, curtailment of travel, mandatory identity cards with photo, black-outs, the list went on and on. All these rules and regulations were posted on a big bulletin board in the center of town.

Everyone had to turn in their radios so people could not listen to the BBC or other allied stations. In its place you were allowed to listen to a simple radio which only had three stations: two Dutch-language German controlled stations, and one in German. The latter often broadcast speeches by Adolf Hitler touting German successes on all fronts. Father turned in one old radio for the record but hid our good radio in the attic so he could listen to the BBC broadcasts from England which were much different from the German ones.

Father worked for a local builder in the early years of the war. The Germans put out a directive in 1941 that all able-bodied men not directly working for the war effort would be put to work on the expansion of the airfield near Leeuwarden, the Frisian capital. The Germans planned a giant fighter plane base to intercept British and American bombers on their bombing missions from England to Germany. They offered extremely high wages so many workers signed up voluntarily. The Germans even offered free bus transportation from every village in the area to the airfield.

Father quit his job at the builder and signed on for the airfield job. After all, there was a family to feed. At first everything went well, the workers enjoyed the one hour bus ride to the airfield picking up men en route and there was a lot of friendly chatter. Many of the workers were unskilled and were put to work with shovels and wheelbarrows. Father was a skilled carpenter and was soon busy building barracks and offices. German supervision was lax and the Dutch workers found plenty of opportunity to sabotage their work.

The Germans were anxious to get the airfield in operation and fighters were flown in from Germany.

The British were recovering from the Blitz and were now organizing bombing raids of their own against Germany. On their route to Germany they had to fly over occupied Holland, or stay to the north of the Dutch offshore islands, and follow the longer route over the North Sea. In either case they were well within reach of the German fighters based in Leeuwarden. When British bombers approached, the alarm sounded and the German fighter pilots scrambled and were in the air in minutes to intercept the enemy. All work was temporarily halted as the fighters took off one after another on the newly constructed runways. Aerial battles often ensued with losses on both sides.

Occasionally some of the British bombers targeted the airfield which took the lives of several Dutch laborers. One of my father's co-workers got hit by shrapnel which took the top of his head off and killed him instantly. Father was only a few feet away from the man and it really shook him up. He refused to go back to work and feigned illness. He did in fact have a stomach ulcer and got a statement from his doctor to that effect excusing him from the airfield job. With the fat paychecks suddenly stopped he started looking into other endeavors.

None of the houses in Bakhuizen, or for that matter most of the municipality, had indoor plumbing and everyone had an outhouse with honey bucket. These barrels with human waste were normally picked up once a week by two men in a municipal truck and the full one was exchanged for an empty one. A barrel of human waste is heavy, and as the outhouses were always in the backyard, it took strong men to carry the full barrels to the truck on the road.

During the last years of the war the trucks could not make their rounds anymore because of lack of fuel and truck parts. This presented a serious problem, something never even remotely considered by us today with flushing toilets which do their job with the flick of a finger. But what would you do if you had honey buckets and nobody came to pick them up? There was only one solution. They had to be emptied and the only available place was the backyard. So Geert, our man in hiding, dug a deep hole in our garden and the first load was laboriously carried out by him and my father and dumped.

Luckily the area has sandy soil and the liquid waste seeped into the ground quite readily and the solids would decompose. This process repeated itself every week when the barrel was full, making sure a previous dumpsite was not disturbed! Little gardening was done anymore as most backyards were small and 'sewage disposal' demanded most of the available area.

After the war when regular municipal pickups were reinstated people could revert to gardening again. The gardens produced bumper crops of vegetables and beautiful flowers. Of course this really was nothing new. The Chinese have used human fertilizer on their fields for millennia. When we emigrated to America after the war we still had no flushing toilets or indoor plumbing.

By 1943 tobacco products were so scarce that many people started growing their own tobacco. It was always believed that it was next to impossible to grow tobacco in Friesland at the 53rd parallel but the sandy soil in our area and warmer than normal summers produced surprisingly good tobacco. Not by Virginia standards perhaps, but for tobacco-starved smokers it was a revelation. It was also a very profitable crop and father saw great opportunities. He enlisted the help of his friends Tjerk and Bart de Blaauw, sons of blacksmith Sibble de Blaauw, who were great mechanics and technically inclined. They designed and built him a tobacco cutting machine which was hand-cranked but could cut large quantities of compressed tobacco leaves in a matter of minutes. It had an automatic feeder which could be adjusted to cut fine shag, pipe tobacco, or chewing tobacco. The original idea to have it power driven by an electric motor was discarded as the power supply was too unevenly distributed. The machine was an immediate success and father was in business again. He was able to use a shed where my grandfather had kept chickens before.

Word spread fast to tobacco growers who now could get their tobacco leaves processed into any product they wanted, even cigars if they so desired. Father read everything he could on tobacco processing and soon was considered an expert in his field. He was hard pressed to keep up with demand. Some farmers delivered seven or eight bags of dried tobacco leaves by horse-drawn wagon and storage became a problem before it could be processed.

My brother and I were also pressed into service 'fermenting' cut tobacco. This entailed hours of cranking a barrel (made of a milk can) with tobacco which had been 'sauced' for flavor (father's secret recipe), on a special stove in a smoky shed. I can still smell the pungent odor of the sauced tobacco, even our clothes smelled of tobacco. George and I took turns cranking the barrel so the tobacco would not burn but kept rotating like the clothes in a modern dryer. We didn't enjoy this job much as it cut into our playing time with our friends, but father just didn't have time for all these chores. He was kept busy at the cutting machine and waiting on customers.

Hans, the commander of the German occupation post, heard that father had tobacco for sale. Father often bought a portion of an especially good batch or traded labor for tobacco. The German tobacco allowance for their troops had dwindled to next to nothing and they were looking for other sources. So they came to father from as far away as Stavoren, where a German garrison was located, and its men bought all they could get their hands on. They paid well and left in good spirits! It was amazing what a little tobacco could do for the mood of a soldier.

The Germans had no inkling that father was deeply involved with the Resistance. Many of the locals thought he was a German sympathizer but the opposite was true.

They looked askance at his activities and considered him a traitor, but father stoically shrugged it off with a touch of cynicism. His apparent friendship with the Germans was just a front and stood him in good stead later on when he needed it most.

Life during World War II was reduced to its simplest forms. The economy came to a virtual standstill and the store shelves were bare. It was a barter economy as money became worthless. It was a struggle just to keep a family fed and clothed. Boys wore short pants and girls wore skirts, usually all hand-me-downs. Everyone wore wooden shoes, leather shoes only on Sunday to church if you were lucky. Boys were rough on wooden shoes, and we often broke the 'cap', the instep portion of the shoe. Father showed us once how to repair a broken cap with bailing wire and from then on we had to do it ourselves. First two grooves had to be sawn over the body and cap of the wooden shoe with a hacksaw, so the wires would be flush. Then we fastened the wire with one nail near the sole and stretched the wire taut over the wooden shoe and cap and nailed it on the opposite side. I got very good at it. Everyone was poor and it was necessary to get the most mileage out of wooden shoes.

The tide of war was slowly turning in favor of the Allies. After Field Marshall Paulus's Sixth Army was annihilated in Stalingrad with the loss of a quarter million men, the Germans never regained the offensive. The drone of airplane engines filled the sky for a good portion of the day now. My friends and I were walking to school on a bright sunny day when we heard and saw the first wave of American bombers approach out of the west on their way to a target in Germany, which in most cases was either Bremen or Hamburg. Four vapor trails coming from each bomber filled the sky with hundreds of long white linear clouds. Multiplied by up to one thousand bombers the cloud thus formed almost blotted out the sun. The planes moved slowly but relentlessly across the sky as if pushed by a giant invisible force which could and would not be stopped. The loud humming drone caused by thousands of engines sounded like millions of bumble bees, a sound I will never forget and which is etched in my mind.

Looking up I saw one of the bombers drop out of the formation make a slow U-turn and head west again. Suddenly the bomb bay doors opened and several bombs were released. We could not hear their howling descent yet but they rapidly gained speed. We hit the ground and waited for the explosions. It wasn't long before closely spaced booms filled the air. We got up and saw a big cloud of dust about half a mile to the southwest. Running as fast as our wooden shoes would carry us we found several large craters. Luckily no one got killed although one of the bombs missed the house of Durk and Willemke Nagelhout by a mere 100 feet.

The plane must have had mechanical problems or have been hit by enemy fire. In either event its crew found it prudent to try to return to England as it could not keep up with the formation.

No one wants war

Liesbeth Gilbert-de Graaff

I was born in Laren near Hilversum and was six years old when the war started. My first memory is that German soldiers took over our Montessori School. The teachers gave all the kids some of the school supplies. So I took some supplies home that we used in first grade math. We had to safely keep those at home until the school was available again.

My father was in jail for six weeks in Amsterdam. I did not understand that because only bad people went to jail. But all the neighbors came to bring us food and they were very nice to my mother, so my dad could not have been a bad guy really. It turned out that he had done something in the Resistance for Jewish people and that the Germans were on to him. But because they could not prove anything he was sent home.

One time the soldiers needed blankets and they went from door to door. Every family had to give them one blanket. My mother gave them the thinnest blanket she could find. On another occasion they needed men. The German soldiers blocked all roads leading from the village and picked up every man who was outside. My father hid under a pile of branches. A soldier came to the pile and my father thought that he had been discovered. But all the soldier did was relieve himself and then he disappeared again. That was also a relief for my father!

Germany also needed leather, so we never got new shoes. The wooden shoe maker in our village was very busy making wooden shoes for all the kids. I remember watching him work in his shop. All the kids wore wooden shoes.

Once the English bombed our village. There was a German barracks just outside the village on the road to Bussum, but a few stray bombs fell on our village. I don't know if anyone got killed but I remember huge craters and damaged houses.

I was always frightened of the sound of the planes flying high overhead on their way from England to Germany because I knew that they carried bombs. And then the air raid sirens would sound and we would have to shelter by the chimney.

My older sister and brother spent some time with farmers in Overijssel. A truckload of children was invited and my brother and sister were among them. It was to strengthen them and make sure they got better food. I do not know how long they were there. After the war when we were teenagers we went to those farmers on our bicycles to thank them. My brother and sister had fond memories of their time there.

I also remember that adults would not talk to kids about the war because there were collaborators who would sometimes ask questions of young children to betray their parents.

Once a young German soldier came to my mother to ask her where my German uncle was hiding. My uncle did not want to work for Hitler. My mother knew nothing of course. When he saw me he said that he had a little girl that looked like me with my braids and my blue eyes. He missed her and asked if I could sit on his lap. I did not want to but my mother felt sorry for him and said: "Go ahead, just for a little while…" I sat on his lap but I thought: 'But he's the enemy…?' He said he did not want war either. As adults we understand better that all people are the same, regardless of race, country or language. No one wants war.

Scary times

Ralph Schotsman

I was almost eight years old on May 10, 1940, the day Germany invaded Holland. At that time we lived in Harderwijk. Mother sent us to school but it was closed. Later our Christian School was taken over by the Germans and so we moved from one school to another, often only for half days of classes. When there was an air raid we would shelter under our benches or lie down in the hallway. Sometimes we even had enough time to go into a concrete shelter.

As a young boy I was often very scared. In the latter part of the war allied bombers and fighter planes would go over our town at night time and towards the very end of the war even in daylight. The terrible drone of the heavy planes kept you from sleeping.

At one time, it must have been 1944, a Lancaster bomber came over our home in flames and crashed close by in a farmer's field. Luckily it had already dropped its bombs, it got shot down by the Germans on the way home. It came down so low that the treetops were burned. Our dad said: "From now on we will go to sleep in one room downstairs so that if this happens again we will all die together."

There were also many air raids on the highway we lived on as well as on the train station and harbor. We used to run for cover. Those were scary times. When the war was over it was a real blessing to sleep at night in peace.

I remember...

Freddi Bousema Weston

I remember... waking up in the middle of the night in our Haarlem home to a very loud droning sound that went on and on. I was four and a half years old. I ran to my parents' room. My father was a sergeant in the Army and he woke my mother up. We opened the window to see what was happening and realized that the sound came from the sky. Other people were also outside or hanging out of their windows. The sky was pitch dark, only a few streetlamps provided some illumination.

I remember... a few days later standing with my mother on Market Square watching German soldiers march into our city with tanks and other equipment. The first few years were fairly uneventful for a child although there were many new rules and restrictions imposed by the occupiers.

I remember... notices plastered around town demanding the populace turn in all gold and silver, radios and bicycles. Of course this was immediately resisted and as little as possible was submitted. If nothing was turned in, raids would be organized to search people's homes. My dad remembered how to make a 'crystal set' radio which was hidden in the ceiling of one of our living room cupboards. I also remember the motif from Beethoven's Fifth Symphony that indicated the latest war news broadcast from London in Dutch.

I remember... that my mother always used a steam cooker - four pans that fitted together covered with a double walled hood - that could cook a whole meal of meat, potatoes, vegetables, soup, all at once on only two inches of water. When all utilities were rationed and later cut off and fuel was scarce or inferior, my dad had someone make a small round stove slightly bigger than the steam cooker, which was then placed on the coal stove heating the living room and small pieces of wood and twigs would do the job of cooking meals.

I remember... being sent out to the Zandvoort Avenue in the suburb of Overveen with my doll carriage to look for branches and twigs to feed the little stove. That stove worked like a charm, even heated the living room a bit, at least the area a few feet around it.

I remember... that IJmuiden was evacuated by the Germans and we ended up with some evacuees assigned to us, two adults and two children who were distant relatives. They occupied one upstairs bedroom and of course this was not a happy situation for anybody. Two women sharing one kitchen, never a good idea.

I remember... that the father rigged up his bicycle to make a generator. Someone just had to 'ride' the stationary bike all night so they could play cards! We had a black out and almost got into big trouble as our 'guests' ignored it and had the balcony doors wide open in the evening. Luckily the police just gave us a warning. I do not remember them staying with us for long, maybe they found better accommodation or perhaps went back to another part of IJmuiden.

I remember… that one day on my way to school on my scooter I was stopped a few blocks from school by German soldiers and was not allowed to proceed. I waited and waited, I heard shooting and later learned that seven or nine hostages had been executed in retaliation for sabotage by the Resistance. The shooting took place right in front of my school.

My school was later occupied by German soldiers and our classes started to take place in private homes here and there in a hit and miss fashion. I took advantage of this to play hooky and hide out at my grandparents' place. My aunt who looked after them, did not mention my visits to my parents. I must have told her a good story. Of course I would get caught sooner or later. It was later, at a point where I had missed most of the year and was set to fail grade 4! As a punishment I had to spend my entire summer catching up and walking clear across town twice a week to have my work checked. I could have gone on to the next level but it was thought I needed to be taught a lesson and do grade 4 all over again! (I was unable to finish my last year of secondary school before we left for Canada after the war due to this indiscretion).

Many people were involved in the 'Underground' as the Resistance Movement was referred to. Of course it was not much discussed, even among friends, as this was very risky business. Even my parents Jan and Riek were involved to some extent. We often provided a 'safe house' for young Resistance fighters on the run who would move from house to house for safety reasons. Being an only child at the time, I was privy to much secret information that I would think twice about divulging to an eight year old child, but my parents told me they trusted me completely not to tell. Of course I had been warned that if I ever told a soul, the soldiers would come and pick up my dad and he would be shot before our eyes! That was a powerful incentive to keep my mouth shut. Not being able to have playmates over or visit them because of security also made it easier.

I remember… coming home one night from a trip with my mother and rushing to get home before eight o'clock when the curfew started. I was talking about something that was sensitive perhaps when mom said: "Sshhh, the walls have ears!"

Sometimes it was safer to have a child pass information than an adult. Late one night, just before curfew, I was sent to an address with a pamphlet with the status of the war and a picture of the Queen with her little girls that had been found somewhere. I was told to go inside the house, hand over the material, wait at least ten minutes and hurry back home before eight p.m.

As the war went on notices went out that all men between 18 and 40 were to report to a certain point to be transported to Germany to work for the war machine. Of course not many showed up so whole neighborhoods were raided for delinquents. My father being of the targeted age group had to go into hiding. He had anticipated this and months earlier had made a hiding place under the house. He made an opening in the kitchen floor under the linoleum and also one in our living room behind the couch hidden by the carpet. There was a space under the house about two and a half feet deep with a sandy floor. So when our neighborhood was being searched it was time to access his hiding place. However, when he opened the trapdoor he found that there was about four inches of water! We quickly gathered anything we could find to keep him out of the water: carpeting, mats, planks, broomsticks, cushions, blankets, anything. He had to go in there. He did, and held a metal garbage can lid over his chest, as the soldiers were known to shoot through floors or ceilings.

I was sent out on my scooter to scout where the soldiers were and what was going on. I would come back and tell dad through the floor that they got Mr. So-and-so, and which street they were combing at that moment! They never came to our street. Unfortunately having lain in the water all day my dad got a kidney infection which was very serious in those days when you could not go out to see a doctor. A doctor was found who would come to our house and could be trusted. My father did recover after a long time. Another time when my father had to go into hiding he ended up at the little house where his elderly parents lived. He and his younger brother had made a hiding place in a bulkhead in their living room. The opening was obscured by a painting.

My aunt, my dad's sister, had a boyfriend, Guus. He was a German orphan from World War I and one of a large number of orphaned children who came to Holland after that war to be raised by Dutch families. But he was still German. He was conscripted by the Germans to serve on the Eastern Front and shipped to Russia. Of course he had no loyalty to the Germans at all and managed to desert and make his way back home to Holland. Of course he also had to go into hiding.

I remember… that my parents and I went to Utrecht one day to visit him. I had not been told about our destination and when I saw him I jumped up and screamed, 'Uncle Guus!'. Of course I was shushed right away as he was no longer called Guus! He had a new identity.

I remember... earlier on in the war when food was starting to get scarce, my parents and I would go by train to Brabant with a suitcase and travel from farm to farm to trade goods for food. Girls of my mother's generation would accumulate a trousseau before they married. This often consisted of twelve of everything – twelve sheets, pillowcases, tablecloths, hand towels, dishtowels etcetera, all neatly kept with ribbons. Of course a lot of these items were still brand new and they made good barter material, just like lengths of cloth to sew dresses. We bartered those for butter, milk, eggs and such.

I escaped with my life

Anne Hendren

Gradually the German occupation began to change our lives. Rationing of food products started during the summer of 1940. Every Sunday morning Pap would rush downstairs to grab our newspaper, De Telegraaf. The headlines were always bad and got worse each week. Every Sunday a new group of merchandise, groceries, or textiles was added to the ration cards. Protein products, meat, butter, and milk were targeted first for the simple reason that those products were all being shipped to Germany. Slowly but surely Holland was being strangled as its food supply was looted so that the occupying forces could live off what the industrious Dutch people had produced.

New laws came into effect with Jewish people being a special target. One of my Jewish classmates came to school one day with a yellow star on her coat. A few weeks later she disappeared never to be seen again. No gatherings of more than five people were allowed. Boy Scouts, Girl Guides, and any group other than Nazi-affiliated youth groups were forbidden to wear uniforms. I was approached by a former Girl Guides leader to help form a small group which would be trained in first aid, rescue work, and later also in emergency operations. We met after hours in a local bank building. The Girl Guides' leader was the manager of that bank and the bank had a nicely concealed back entrance. Later all of our training would come in very handy. We wore our Guides' scarves outside as a head scarf. That was our secret sign and there was no law against wearing a blue head scarf!

All of my high school years in Utrecht were during the war. I often wished that I could go back in time and redo those years under normal circumstances. My high school was a very old building with large classrooms, high ceilings and huge windows. The program I followed consisted of French, German, English, Greek, Latin, Science, Advanced Math, Chemistry, Geography, History, Drawing, and P.E. giving access to university after graduation. The Germans immediately decreed that there had to be more emphasis on the German language and less on English. My German teacher was a lovely old lady, very kind but strict and an excellent instructor. She used to teach us lots of old German songs, ballads, and fairy tales. She never tried to push German politics and did not try to minimize our Dutch heritage. Because she made it so much fun we did not come to hate the German language. We also had a marvelous teacher for English and I became very proficient in that language.

By 1943 the war intensified. The United States had now joined the fight. The rules and regulations in the occupied countries became even more stifling and rigid. English and American music was not allowed to be played on the radio. The cheerful-sounding Dutch street organs disappeared. There was less and less to eat, especially in winter. We had a small plot in a community garden (similar to a victory garden) on which we tried to grow some vegetables and potatoes. This garden was located next to the huge bridge that crossed the Amsterdam-Rhine Canal, a major waterway. Many times English fighter planes and bombers tried to bomb the bridge. It was my job to tend our garden. To get there I had to ride my bicycle across that bridge.

On one such afternoon the English planes came and German guards on the bridge shot at the planes with machine guns. Bombs and gunfire were all over the bridge and the noise was deafening. I lay flat on the ground, trembling with fear and with my heart in my throat. The fight seemed to last for hours. When it was over I raced to my bike and rushed across that scary bridge fearing another attack any minute. I sighed in relief once I safely reached home.

They both hit me

Caty de Graaf

I n 1943 or 1944 we were playing outside in the street around the corner when one of the bigger boys said "hey, it's past eight p.m. our curfew time." We all ran home. My little brother made it home but I did not. One of our neighbors pulled me inside their home. At the other end of the street which was quite long stood two drunken German solders with their rifles ready to shoot. The neighbors lived upstairs and they had a spy mirror outside their window so they could look down the street both ways. It looked like a sort of side mirror on the cars of today. When the coast was clear I went home. I had to enter a small hallway that led straight past what we called the nice room. My father was standing in the doorway and for the first time in my young life, I was about eight, he hit me. I had to go around the corner into the big hallway where my mother was standing in the living room doorway and she hit me. I had to run through the kitchen and sunroom, I had to pass either my mom or dad again to go upstairs, forgot who I chose but they hit me again. Neither ever hit any of their children before or after this incident. Today I understand it was because they were afraid that I could have been hurt or worse.

We had two men hidden under the kitchen floor (I heard them knocking once, my mom told me it was the neighbors) and we had the English radio channel and weapons, so my parents were particularly concerned about attracting unnecessary attention.

Memory glimpses

Enno Reckendorf

Sitting on the pavement, legs dangling over the dynamited draw of the New Bridge. Sunny morning, May 10, 1940. I was 10.

Listening to older students at Quaker School Eerde near Ommen talking about our music teacher being interned by the Germans. His mother was English.

Jewish students and teachers had to form a separate school in an off-campus dormitory. My father was among them.

Easter vacation in Friesland at a roommate's house. When I returned, mother, tired of house-parenting at the school, had moved to an 1861 brick farm house and father rejoined us. She set up a textile studio and he made wooden toys in a cleaned-up chicken coop.

That summer I learned to sail at Grouw. When I returned my sister had scarlet fever. After her ear operation I visited her often at Sofia Hospital isolation ward in Zwolle, where I stood outside her window. She was not yet four.

While visiting Amsterdam I watched the spectacle of search lights and flak during an air raid. Shrapnel clattering down on the street, a burning bomber spinning down slowly onto the Carlton Hotel downtown. Smoky fire.

Allied night bomber shot down, burnt in pasture near our house. Men removed remains of crew member with large wads of cotton. Followed horse-drawn, open sided black hearse to village cemetery. German soldiers fired volleys over the grave. Huge crowd, totally quiet.

One fall the occupiers forced closure of the Eerde schools. The Jewish students and teachers went to concentration camps Vught or Westerbork, some went into hiding. I was sent to school in Zwolle, a half-hour train ride away.

British escort-fighter plane shot down nearby. Machinegun barrels sticking out of wings, engine and cockpit burned, plane looked small. We often saw lots of airplanes. Four miles up.

That winter I caught pneumonia. Sulfa pills.

Spring 1944: Father was called up for forced labor on the West Wall. He went into hiding instead. Visited him stealthily, two villages away.

June 7 or 8, 1944, passing a news stand on the way to school I asked a friend, "Hans, what is an invasion?"

Chaotic interruptions
of high school education

Robert Colyn

We received our high school education in Haarlem at the Christian Lyceum under very trying circumstances. In 1941 the German army ordered various high schools in our area to vacate their buildings so they could be used as barracks for their troops. These events led to chaotic interruptions in our academic training. Our school was not the first one in our town to be taken over by the occupying army, a Catholic high school for boys was. Our principal Dr. Joost van der Elst, being a good Dutch patriot, offered the favor to his Catholic colleague of sharing our school building with the students of his school. This was certainly an admirable cooperative gesture in times of disorder but undoubtedly resulted in study conditions not conducive to effective learning for most students of either school.

Our normal weekly school program was split in half. Class time was shortened by about 50%. Our school occupied the building in the morning, the Catholic boys in the afternoon after we had vacated the building. These boys soon started enjoying their stay in our classrooms. Being curious who was occupying their seat during the morning hours they left notes to the unknown occupant of their desk probing for his or her identity. Once it was discovered that a female student shared his desk, the student's testosterone became more activated, causing him to seek further and more intimate contact with his

(Protestant) penpal. Once this furtive 'get-to-know-each-other-better' correspondence struck paydirt the floodgates opened up, resulting in wild adolescent love letters between the two denominations.

The Catholic principal, becoming aware of this interfaith exchange of statements of passion, decided to put a stop to this unholy activity. He threatened to discipline any sinner of his own flock caught in the lusty act of contacting his counterpart on the other side of the religious divide. Now that the 'line in the sand' was drawn by his Catholic counterpart, our principal also felt compelled to issue a warning against this frivolous activity, advising our girls to end their amorous flirtations by pen.

It became abundantly clear to us high school students that school attendance would be governed by the whim of the Nazi authorities. One year after the Catholic school had moved in with us, in 1942, those authorities decided to occupy our school as well kicking both school populations out onto the street. It became a great challenge for both principals and their school boards to find new classroom accommodations again for a few thousand students somewhere in the city or its suburbs. But somehow they succeeded in relocating all of us in many separate and much smaller buildings, spread out throughout the area, seriously complicating the job of teaching for the faculty and school administration.

I moved to a vacated private villa in Aerdenhout (a plush suburb of Haarlem) known as the Viersprong (The Four Ways) located at a crossroads. This patrician home had been beautifully decorated inside with oak paneling and the owner must have been an affluent person to afford such extravagance. Our classroom seemed to have been the library of the house. Not a bad place to teach teenagers. This room was now converted to classroom 3g of the high school I attended. It was in this room that I first met my lovely wife-to-be in September of 1942.

In the spring of the following year some officers of the German Afrika Korps (after its recent defeat in North Africa) visited our villa to check it out as a possible accommodation for officers of their unit who had made it back to mainland Europe. Their khaki uniforms and special hats gave them away as General Erwin Rommel's Desert fighters. And yes, of course we were thrown out again!

Again our studies were drastically interrupted before the school year would come to its regular scheduled end. Again we had to move to another building clear on the other side of town where we finally ended the thrice interrupted school year in July of 1943.

The next school year (1943-44) began in September in the same building we had left in July. The Allies had just begun their conquest of Sicily and the Southern part of Italy. We felt that the liberation of Western Europe was around the corner, not foreseeing that this happy moment would not arrive until May 1945, 20 months later. In the spring of 1944 it happened again! We had to move out on orders of the German authorities. Finding another building this time however, became an even more difficult task for our school officials because our principal had just been arrested by the Gestapo and sent to a concentration camp. The authorities had ordered him to supply them with a list of all male students who qualified for slave labor in the German armament industries, but he refused to do so.

Every male in occupied Holland between 18 and 40 years old had to register for the infamous 'Arbeitseinsatz' (Forced Labor) at a nearby employment office. He would then be transported to his destination somewhere in the Third Reich to help keep the Nazi war machine going. German armies were stretched out over a huge area: from the Arctic tundras in Norway and Finland to the Sahara Desert in North Africa, and from the English Channel to the Volga river in southern Russia. Most German men were recruited for duty in the Armed Forces to do the fighting for Hitler, leaving noticeable shortages in the German labor force. To fill these shortages the Nazi leaders decided to enslave whoever they could round up in the European countries they had conquered since 1938, and add these victims to their workforce.

For a number of Dutchmen it was not always possible to find a way to go into hiding. Others simply did not have the backbone and fortitude to even try escaping from forced labor. So they ended up in German industrial centers under constant aerial bombardment, facing life threatening dangers day after day. Indeed, many of these forced laborers did not survive the daily destruction of German cities and infrastructure between 1942 and 1945.

Dr. van der Elst who was until then known for his compliant stance regarding Nazi orders (for the obvious reason of keeping his already crippled school program running as long as he possibly could) had felt he could not comply with this latest Nazi request. He refused and paid the price for it with his imprisonment!

It was a torturous period for him in a concentration

camp particularly after he was informed that someone less patriotically inclined on the school board had complied with the Nazi request. The consequences were as anticipated. Many students (including myself) had to go into hiding after reaching their 18th birthday. My brother Henk had preceded me in 1942 in this disappearing act, moving away to a remote farm area in the province of Friesland. He remained in hiding until the end of the war.

So in the spring of 1944 our school locality was changed again, although this time the situation was reversed: we moved into a Catholic girls' school run by nuns. It was the Sancta Maria High School located in a stately villa near the city center.

I soon made friends with the Mother Superior of the school because I became aware that she showed much interest in hearing the latest war news from radio London, and she realized with great enjoyment that I could be her illegal news source for the day. She in turn could then spread the (hopefully good) war news to the other nuns. Listening to Allied Forces' broadcasts was strictly forbidden by the Nazis all during the war. Early on in the Nazi occupation, radios had to be turned in to the authorities. Of course many radio owners had no intention of complying with that Nazi order and consequently hid their radio somewhere in a secret place at home. The German authorities were much aware of this defiant attitude and spent a great effort during all five occupation years trying to jam the reception from Radio London. In spite of their noisy interference during the radio broadcasts 24 hours a day, the news came through audibly enough for us illegal listeners.

One had to be very careful in letting others know about this forbidden news source. Anyone caught by the Gestapo would risk their own lives as well as those of others at the place where the radio was found. The home where I had lived since July 1939 housed an illegal radio that my brother had built in 1940. It performed well, keeping all of us in the family informed about the Allied advances toward Nazi Germany on a daily basis.

Mother Superior and I went into her handy little school office (before my classes would start), where under the blessing arms of the Holy Mother statue, I explained with the aid of a school atlas the progress of the latest battles at the Normandy beaches and later General Patton's daring breakthrough to Paris.

She was a feisty nun who expressed her feelings about the Nazi 'Anti-Christ' in no uncertain terms. She did not show much pity towards the Godless Nazi scum surrounding us or dying in the countryside of Normandy. Nor did she seem to be shocked by the continuous aerial bombardment of their Fatherland.

Not allowed to live near the coast

Liesbeth Boysen-van den Blink

'll start my story in May of 1939 in Eindhoven, I just had my ninth birthday and three weeks later my mother died. My two brothers and I were sent to Den Briel to live with my grandparents. It was a big change in more than one way. In Eindhoven we lived outside the city, we bused to school and had few friends. Now everybody lived close by, we walked to school, had friends across the road and somehow, with all the sadness after my mother's death, we were very happy.

We knew about the tensions in the land and the mobilization of the Dutch army. My father who was a doctor was called up to serve with the Dutch Army Red Cross but came to visit us as often as he could.

Then came May 1940, Rotterdam was bombed and burned. We could see this from the attic window. This was the second time I saw my Opa cry.

In 1942 a new decree came out. Nobody was allowed to live near the coast anymore (Hitler was building the Atlantic Wall). The families were moved inland and housed in other people's homes. My grandparents were given 48 hours to vacate their home! Father was their only child so we arrived at my father's doorstep in Eindhoven in the middle of the night with a truck full of belongings, a rooster and seven hens! These had to be housed in the 'coal cupboard' until their coop was built. They were a sight to be seen, all black. My grandparents ended up staying for seven years.

My father remarried and a new baby got added to the group. With an uncle in hiding from the Nazis and at times strangers moving in and out it was busy in our house.

All kinds of things happened in those years but we all have those memories. Father, mother and the baby sister disappeared a few times to hide because the Germans were looking for my Dad.

We were bombed in December of 1942. Unfortunately the English bombed from a high altitude and missed their targets. Usually the RAF were masters in their attacks, they dropped leaflets warning workers to get out of the factories and they usually bombed on Saturday afternoons when the workers were at home.

The nightly air convoys of planes flying over to bomb Germany, that is a noise I still hear when I think back, the constant drone of all the planes going over. When the last ones flew over the first were on their way back.

We had the added attraction of the Sunday bombings. Our house was on a direct approach line to Welschap Airport near Eindhoven. The RAF came over, circled around and on their downward flight they were so low you could see the pilots. This was not scary because we knew they were aiming for the airport.

We heard about D-Day on a radio my dad had in a cookie-tin.

They were buried with their aircraft

Cecil Adema

I n May 1940 we lived in Speers, a village not far from Sneek in Friesland. My twin brother Klaas and I really loved it there. On May 10 and 11 the German soldiers came down the highway on bikes and horses. At that time we were ten years old and our father worked for a dairy farmer.

In 1942 all food was scarce and was only given through food coupons. So my dad said we should move to a mixed farm where we could have plenty of potatoes and grain. One night before we moved my father yelled that we had to come down out of bed. It was extremely noisy outside. A big English bomber flew over our house very low with two of its engines on fire. It circled back around over the house and lost the two engines. Then it flew past two homes and came down in the meadows 500 feet from our house. It burned like hell. There were seven people in the burning aircraft, one from New Zealand, three from Canada, and three Americans. Dead. Only one was found outside the aircraft and the Germans buried him in the cemetery at the neighboring village of Deersum. The rest were buried with their aircraft right there in the meadow.

In May of 1942 we moved to a farm near the town of Tzum. We really enjoyed life there. Because there were no books or pens to write with we only went to school for one and a half years and then they closed the school. So my Dad said we had to help the farmer in the fields during the summer. We had plenty to eat including duck eggs that we found in the fields. The only thing we did not have was wood to warm our food. Most days we would go into the fields and get any branches we could find. The last year, during the winter, it was extremely cold and there were no more trees to find. Every day we went at noon to Tzum to the milk factory where they would warm our food for us and we could take it back home. They always helped us first because we had to walk the farthest, three miles.

In the evenings we would go in the field to steal wood off the bridges to use to warm the house. One day, dad and my brother and I were in the meadows looking for wood, because we had nothing left, and had just arrived at a bridge when an English airplane came over. It dropped a flare lighting the entire meadow so we jumped in a ditch. After 20 minutes it was dark again and Dad did not trust what was going on and took us home. That night we went to bed and around midnight the aircraft came back. It dropped 24 containers of weapons for the Resistance. Dad told us not to go out of the house to help because it was too dangerous. The farmer we stayed with had been hiding a Dutch judge who worked with the Resistance. The judge came to our house and asked us to help gather weapons from two containers that had burst open.

I immigrated to Canada in 1952. Just recently I was told that they were dredging the canal behind my old house and that they found one more container of weapons in the canal and when they opened it up they found that the weapons were like new.

No contact with home

Gerard van der Weyden

I was just seven years old when in May 1940 the German army invaded The Netherlands. My friend Joop and I were playing with a tennis ball at the corner of our Amsterdam city street and were unaware of what was happening. Yes, we had a radio at home but there were no hourly newscasts so we played in blissful ignorance.

That changed soon though when we heard aircraft overhead. From our bedroom windows we watched and saw little planes fight each other by turning, going up and down and shooting. Some had circular markings and others had black crosses. We could see tracer bullets and they hit each other. Black smoke emanated from the fuselage and we could see fire. Parachutes opened and little figures drifted to the ground. This took place a fair distance away from us, over Schiphol airport to the south of the city, so we were not afraid.

Life went on. My parents had eight children. I was number three in the sequence. My eldest sibling was three years older than I.

Food supply became a problem and from time to time one or two of us were sent to eat with people who owned a grocery store. There we were served meals we certainly did not see at home. I had a food distribution card but never did see it.

During our six week summer vacation we were sent to farms. I stayed at a small farm and learned a lot about cows, pigs, chickens, manure, wood chopping, oats, barley, rye, potatoes etcetera. I would have never learned about those except for the war.

I ate my morning porridge together with thirty or so flies that lined up on my plate around the edge of the porridge.

At night I worked my way up the ladder to the bedroom where I shared a bed with the farmer's son who was in his twenties. We had to wash at a pump which delivered cold water only.

At the farm things were going on that were not talked about. I would see someone but it appeared that that person did not exist. Much later we understood that these people were hiding from the Germans.

In the fall of 1944 the four eldest children were lined up and readied for a trip away from Amsterdam. On a flatbed truck with trailer we drove east and crossed a bridge over the river IJssel just before it closed at eleven p.m. We were huddled in blankets and hungry. We had left home at one p.m. Just before the town of Raalte near Zwolle the truck got a flat tire and as there was no spare we walked three kilometers in the dark to a church where we were bedded down on straw.

The next morning we all got a slice or two of very dark rye bread.

We reached our destination of Gramsbergen that day. We were made to sit in a large room. People came, looked us over and then picked someone. My eldest brother went to a big farm. My second eldest brother ended up with a teacher, my sister with a doctor and I was not picked so I stayed where I was and that was with the Protestant minister of the town.

I learned how to polish big boots, set the breakfast table and sow spinach in the small garden. At times a dark figure was seen in the hall and that was 'Frits the Hobo', an alias for the reverend Slomp, a national leader in the Resistance movement.

We spent roughly half a year in Gramsbergen. There was no contact with our family at home and I can only guess how our parents must have felt, what with half their brood out of touch, no mail, no telephone.

During the occupation:

I experienced lice and got some forty ulcers on my hands and neck.

I learned to speak a dialect while I was evacuated.

I saw armadas of aircraft flying overhead.

I saw searchlights at night weaving and catching a plane where their beams crossed. I learned the use of manure on the fields - boy do I still wash and clean potatoes today because of it.

I dropped a pan of precious soup from the soup kitchen on the ground, for which I had stood in line for over an hour, my mother got down on her knees to scrape it up.

I saw bombs being dropped.

I saw rifles stuck in the ground with helmets on top where soldiers had been hastily buried.

I saw Jewish people being rounded up and their furniture and belongings being hauled away the next day by Verhulst Moving Company.

Today, I will not wait in line for anything. I stood in so many lines during the war for food. I will not waste food as during the war we ate every scrap and licked our plates. I remember hunger. I remember my father's sad face after days of cycling to find food at farms and returning with very little.

My mind goes on edge when I hear the German language being spoken. The enemy was with me for five years and their marching songs and shouts like 'Achtung' cannot be erased from memory.

Our family adapts to the occupation

Kees Vermeer

During the first years of the German occupation of The Netherlands from 1940 to 1943, the Dutch tried to carry on with life as normally as possible. In 1943 when the war started to turn against the Germans, food conditions grew worse as most of the Dutch grain and dairy production was transported to Germany. My family lived in Gorinchem, then a small city of about 15,000 inhabitants, situated on the Merwede river. Gorinchem is surrounded by earthen city walls and gates from the 1600s which are still beautifully preserved.

In 1943 I was twelve and lived with my retired parents, two sisters, Cato and Ali, and my brother Jan (all in their twenties) on a street called Emma Street. It was part of a suburb called the 'Nieuwe Hoven', which was located outside the city walls.

Since my father was a well-liked retired school principal from Noordeloos, a small village in the Alblasserwaard, we had ready access to dairy products from the farmers there. My sisters and I often biked to Noordeloos to buy milk, butter and cheese. Because of this fortunate access to a good supply of dairy we also shared with neighbors in dire need.

One neighbor was a Jewish lady across the street, who had to wear a yellow star, but hardly dared to come out of her house because of the risk of being picked up and sent to Germany. She survived the war and expressed her gratitude many years after when I visited Holland from Canada.

Although we had sufficient access to dairy products, we still lacked warm clothes during cold winters, other foodstuffs than dairy, footwear and heating fuel. The whole family, except my father who we thought deserved respect in his retirement, became mobilized to produce woolen sweaters, underwear and socks. We turned to the past to see how wool was made and Jan constructed two beautiful spinning wheels for Cato and Ali. My sisters visited sheep farmers in the Alblasserwaard to obtain the raw wool. A barter was made as money had lost much of its pre-war value: the farmer would get half of the spun wool and my sisters kept the other half.

At home it was like a factory. My sisters spun wool all day and my mother made woolen sweaters, socks and underwear. I had a slight role in the process: I transported the wool between my sisters and the farmers once contact had been established. I also was a willing guinea pig to wear any wool product my mother made regardless of its outcome or shape. Most of her products were excellent and suited the need, but my mother had some other ideas of her own. She thought the war could last many years and I was young and undoubtedly would grow. The result was that I wore very baggy sweaters and underwear which had room for many years of growth. I readily adapted and rolled up the long and flabby woolen undershirts at waist level under my shirt, baggy sweaters or pants, whatever was suitable under the circumstances. The funny bulges at my waist did not bother me except on one occasion. In the summer I stayed for a few weeks with my cousin Sye, and his wife in Lisse. As Lisse was not far from the sea, Sye and I biked one day to the nearest beach. The beach was full of sunbathing people. Since there was little privacy Sye and I undressed as quickly as possible. Next thing I knew was Sye choking with laughter while rolling in the sand. I felt all eyes were on me. After I took off my pants my bulging undershirt had unfolded and rolled way down to my ankles right on the beach. I felt so embarrassed. The incident made a lasting impression on Sye as he still talked about it when I met him many years after in Canada.

We adapted to the food situation (other than dairy) in various ways. In 1944, when there was a shortage of all sorts of commodities, we looked at every opportunity to provide for our needs. Cato and Ali traded spun wool and textiles for wheat with the farmers. The textiles were acquired from my brother, Gys, who had a textile store in Hoornaar, a village near Noordeloos. Textiles became scarcer as the war progressed. By 1944 Gys had little left to sell but he stored sufficient stock to barter for other commodities. Unfortunately, that abruptly came to an end when late in 1944 lightning hit the roof of the house of a nearby friendly farmer who had stashed most of Gys's textiles in the attic. The textiles were all burned. There was a much worse fate at that same farm that year. The Landwacht (uniformed Dutch Nazi sympathizers) betrayed five people hiding from the Nazis, who lived in a room inside a haystack. They were rounded up and shot.

My sisters were excellent barterers for wheat and my mother baked delicious bread. Like with milk, we brought loaves of bread to neighbors in need, as my mother was a very generous woman.

Later bread baking became difficult when we were no longer allowed to use electricity. If caught using it one would be severely punished. My mother used a gas stove for cooking instead. To overcome the problem, Jan set up a stationary bicycle in our attic. A small generator was attached to the bicycle and connected to car batteries. We all took turns riding the bicycle to create electricity. With our electricity we lit carbide lamps. At the same time Jan inserted a needle through a tiny hole in the house electricity meter located in a small box near the front door. The needle stopped the meter from running while we used electricity to the fullest extent. The threat of punishment if caught did not deter us. The set up was partly a cover up in case we were checked by a meter reader or the German Police. The German Police took over several houses on the adjacent block of our street. One day, Germans visited our house suddenly. We were able to pull out the needle before we opened the front door and fortunately my mother was not baking bread at the time.

Jan worked as a mechanic for a car garage in Gorinchem. Most of the repair during the last war years was on German army trucks. There were not many privately owned vehicles left at that time. Jan used the opportunity to steal food from the trucks brought in for repair. He often brought home stolen food. But once Jan was caught taking a large bag of peas from a German truck. He was pistol whipped by the German who caught him in the act and was imprisoned in the cellar of the municipal hall. We were very worried our house would be searched as Jan was a member of the Dutch Resistance. He had stored weapons underneath the floor of our front room. The storage place was accessible through a sawed-out piece of the wooden floor covered with a carpet with a sofa on top. Cato visited Jan's employer to discuss how to get Jan out of prison. Cato and the employer came up with a brilliant idea. The employer talked to the Germans in charge and convinced them that Jan was an excellent mechanic, and that without him, many of the German trucks could not be repaired. Besides being a mechanic, the employer indicated that Jan was somewhat crazy and didn't understand the consequences of taking food from the trucks he repaired. Within three days Jan was released and was back to repairing German trucks in the garage, but he continued to take every opportunity to steal food from the Germans.

Bicycles were a precious commodity during the war as there was little else for transportation for the Dutch population. During the last years of the occupation the Germans confiscated bicycles from the Dutch as they needed them too.

At one time I walked through the city gate at Arkel Street (one of the two main entrances to the old city) when a German soldier confiscated a bicycle from a citizen. The owner grabbed the bicycle from the soldier's hands and dashed with his bicycle in hand up the earthen city wall. The soldier shouted at the man to stop and leant his automatic machine gun on the railing of a small bridge nearby for support. He fired several salvos at the desperate fleeing man. As I stood within ten steps of the soldier I held my breath. There were only the two of us, the soldier and me, at the scene.

Everyone else had run away. I was too fascinated by the fleeing man's courage to think of leaving. Fortunately, the man was not hit by bullets as he wildly zigzagged on his bicycle. This is the only time in my whole life that I witnessed a man risking his life for a bicycle. Of course it was a foolish act, but I greatly admired the man for his courage.

Each member of our family except my mother had a bicycle. But by the end of 1943, there was only one left in our household as we ran out of tires and the Germans had confiscated several of them. I did not abandon my bicycle after the tires were gone but continued to ride it without tires between school and home until the wheels collapsed.

Riding a tireless bicycle made a hell of a noise. One of the teachers at the Home Economics school near our house used me as a clock: when she heard me come home for lunch she would stop giving lessons to have lunch too. After the bike collapsed, Jan gave me another one with good tires for which I was extremely grateful. After all, a boy without a bicycle feels lost in Holland.

Jan was a bike snatcher par excellence. His own was confiscated by the Germans and he was given a useless coupon in return. The coupon was a promissory note indicating that the owner would receive a bicycle after the war was over. Jan soon replaced his confiscated bicycle with another from the Germans. He used a clever strategy to steal them. He did this only in the vicinity of our church. He would watch a German soldier leave his bicycle outside a building near the church. If the conditions were right he would steal the bicycle quickly and hide it in the vestibule of our church. No German would look for stolen bicycles in a church. He would leave the bicycle for a day or two and after that he would calmly ride it home. My sisters, Jan and I all had our bicycles replaced in this manner. We felt great, we got even with the Germans in such a just manner. Best of all was that we could ride again.

In the summer of 1944 I committed a blunder. I am not proud of the incident, but I tell the story as it beautifully demonstrates the instant reaction and adaptation by my family to the situation.

At that time the Home Economics School for girls was taken over by the Germans for use as a field hospital. Massive and horrible German war casualties were brought to the hospital. Dutch women were employed there who dated German soldiers. Dating German soldiers was detested by the Dutch and the women paid for it after the war. On one occasion two of those women walked down our street towards the hospital. I called out "traitors". The women got upset and dragged me towards the hospital.

To make matters worse, my mother, who saw the incident through the window, ran out of the door and shouted "You nasty women! Leave the boy alone!". The women cowered and immediately let me go. Not long after the incident, I was in our backyard, when Ali suddenly appeared on the balcony. She frantically waved to me to flee as the Germans had come to the front door. I immediately knew what was coming so I jumped over the back fence, ran across the field behind our home, entered alleys between other houses and moved through backyards behind walls and vegetation, crossed several roads until I reached a haystack at a farm nearby. My heart pounded heavily from the effort.

It was hours later when a friend who had seen me flee called out that it was safe to return home.

In the meantime, my family suffered the consequences of my name calling. When two Germans entered our home, they asked for the 'boy'. My family replied that I had fled and that they did not know my whereabouts.

The Germans threatened to take my father instead if I would not be home in half an hour. Then they left.

Well, what to do? My sister, Cato, consulted a lawyer for advice. The lawyer told her that under no circumstances the 'boy' should return home as he could be severely beaten or killed.

My brother Jan contacted our neighbor next door who was a cement contractor. He had considerable influence with the Germans as he helped them build their bunkers. He also spoke German fluently. Our neighbor came to our house immediately to await the return of the Germans. He was a gentle man, but could not resist the temptation of money and business from the Germans. Only one German returned to our house to ask for the 'boy' again. This was fortunate as it was easier to handle one than two soldiers. With two, they would not let their guard down as one checks the other.

My family told the soldier that I was just a little boy. The soldier asked for my age. My mother replied that I was 10 (actually I was 13) and showed him a photo of when I was 10 years old. Our neighbor asked the soldier to sit down, to make himself comfortable and asked if he had a family of his own in Germany. The soldier put his hand in his pocket and pulled out a wallet with a photo of his wife and two young children. He shed some tears and said he had not seen them in a long time. The conversation went on for some time, after which the soldier stood up. He said he would not take the case any further but warned my family that if the 'boy' behaved badly again, there would be severe consequences. After that he left. My family expressed their gratitude to our neighbor. I returned home expecting severe punishment from my family but they were so relieved and happy that they forgot about it.

We had two different types of people who shared our home for eight months during the German occupation. I call them 'guests' although they were not real guests in the literal sense of that word. One type were the people hiding from the Germans, who came first and the other, a German tank crew, who came later.

The first person hiding from the Germans who stayed with us for four months during the first half of 1944, was a heavy-set, middle-aged man. He was a diver with the Dutch Navy. He was not a great joy to me. Although his wife lived in Gorinchem, we were told he was in hiding from the Germans and so his wife could not be told where he was. We soon found out that the woman who walked in the park next to our house each weekend and who wiped her eyes with a handkerchief, was his wife.

The man was given my bedroom next to the park and I had to sleep in the attic. The attic was a dark place with a small loft window. At night, when I went upstairs, I sang loudly as I was afraid of the dark and ghostly atmosphere. That scary feeling was made worse by the drying and rotting tobacco leaves hanging from the beams supporting the roof, which gave the space the appearance of a jungle. I stooped underneath the leaves and ran to my bed at the other end of the attic where I dove under the blanket. That ghostly atmosphere left such an impression on me that many years later, when I visited my mother in Holland, I still sang loudly during a night visit to the old attic.

The tobacco leaves belonged to my father who was the only smoker in the family. He had long run out of pipe tobacco and cigars, so he grew his own tobacco in our backyard. A lot of the leaves did not dry properly in the attic, but being an addict, he smoked them anyway. And so did his cronies, mainly retired school principals and teachers, who sought my father's company, partly for his tobacco.

When they were at our place, the whole room was full of smoke and fungoid tobacco smell. I could hardly talk for several days after. I did not know then that I was allergic to tobacco smoke. I never blamed my father for smoking, as at that time he wasn't aware of the health consequences, lung and stomach cancer, from which he died.

There was another reason I did not enjoy the company of our 'guest'. He spied and tattled on me. He had seen from his window upstairs that a girl kissed me in the park. I was not aware that he had seen us but he raised the topic at the dinner table. He told my family he had seen me with a girl. I felt uneasy but tried to look as indifferent as I could while eating my meal. He continued on with the topic for some time to obtain further details but I did not respond. Even my family remained silent. My unease changed to annoyance that he, as a guest, brought up the topic at the table. I broke the silence and the spell that he had cast when I asked him to pass the potatoes.

The man in hiding was a voracious eater and went through large helpings of potatoes. He became a serious burden on our food resources. His needs for large quantities of food may have been the main reason he was lodging with us. It was also the main reason we asked the Resistance to find someone else to take care of him. Our wish was granted and the burden lifted. Needless to say, I jumped for joy when I returned to my own bedroom.

The second 'guest' stayed with us for two months during the fall of 1944. He was about 20 and hailed from Groningen, where his family owned a small aviation business. Jan got him a job at the garage where he worked. Unfortunately he had 'sticky fingers'. Jan had saved some money in a cigar box up in the attic.

One Sunday, after we had all returned from church, Jan noticed some money was missing but he did not know how much. So Jan counted the bills and wrote down the serial numbers. The next Sunday after church more bills had disappeared, and now Jan knew exactly how many and which bills were missing.

Jan confronted the man. I was not present at the confrontation but I understand it was quite a scene. Jan put the cigar box on the dining table an asked the fellow if he had seen the box before. Initially he denied it but after some prodding he admitted to having seen the box before. Jan told him he was the only one who could have taken the money. Again the man initially denied it, but later admitted he had taken some money. Jan asked him how much. The fellow mentioned a certain amount. Jan replied it was more than that. His adversary mentioned a bigger amount, but Jan replied that he had taken more. I understand this went on for some time, until the fellow broke down and admitted the full stolen amount. His family was contacted and the next morning he was picked up by his father who apologized profusely. The fellow was perhaps not truly in need of a hiding place. His habits may have been a major problem for his father's business.

One December night in 1944, a tremendous noise next to my bedroom woke me up with a bolt. The house was shaking from what seemed to be an increasing roar of engines. There were shouting German voices and trees and shrubs were crashing in the adjacent park. I carefully pushed aside the curtain and saw tanks being parked among the trees.

The next morning there were four tanks next to our house. They likely were parked there for cover from air attacks. Camouflage nets were draped over the tanks. The large Red Cross sign on the roof of the nearby field hospital may have provided extra protection from an aerial attack.

We were soon contacted by German officers who looked around our house. They wanted our back room, the main sitting and dining room, for the tank crew. The smaller front room (with Jan's weapons underneath), the small kitchen and all of upstairs were left to us. We were very happy our whole house was not taken over.

About eight soldiers used the back room. They slept in old arm chairs and on mattresses on the floor for the next two months. The soldiers, mostly 20 year olds, were no burden to us. They went their own way and we ours. As we encountered them each day we initially greeted them politely and after some time, engaged them in conversation. This was a first for us.

We had never talked of our own accord to German

soldiers before as we hated everything they stood for. For example, if a soldier asked for directions, we pointed the other way. This was the attitude of most Dutchmen. When Germans marched through a street in Gorinchem and sang 'We will sail against England', most people turned their backs to the marching column or disappeared from the street. Boys sometimes would call out 'Splash, Splash, Splash' at the end of their marching song, suggesting they would drown before reaching England. I was somewhat more anti-German than most Dutch boys, feelings instilled by my fiercely independent family. For instance once when a group of boys including me looked curiously at the tanks for the first time a soldier offered candies. All boys accepted them, except me. The soldier felt offended and tried to force a candy in my mouth without success. But when he left, I stole candy from the tank.

After two weeks we conversed with most of the tank crew who lived with us. They were bright, educated, and a cheerful bunch. They may have belonged to an elite group although they definitely were not SS. We were not afraid of them. We joked and even told them they would soon lose the war. They laughed about that too and replied "So what, we'll go home." They asked me questions like "Are there any girls around?".

At Christmas they all sang carols until midnight. We listened quietly in the front room. We had considered them before to be an aberrant and a devious race of the human species. Now we realized they were not all highly disciplined and technically advanced monsters but people with feelings like us. At the beginning of February they and their tanks suddenly disappeared. I understand they made a counterattack across the big rivers to the south where the Allied forces were. Less than half the crew and only two of the four tanks returned to the park. Some of the survivors had lost an arm or a leg. They did not return to our house. I asked one survivor I met on the street where the others were but he avoided my question and looked dispirited. This was the first time I felt sorry for German soldiers.

In retrospect, I cannot help but compare the relationships we had with the two men in hiding and the tank crew. It is ironic that I only have unpleasant memories of the people our family tried to help and made extensive sacrifices for, while of the German tank crew I have no bad memories at all. The feeling of hate for the German occupation and its absence for the tank crew, when they no longer behaved like the enemy, puzzled me for some time. The puzzle was resolved when I began to understand that the feeling of hate is only as strong as one allows it to be.

Contributors

John Eyking
John lives in Millville, Nova Scotia.

Roland Krijgsman
Roland Krijgsman was born in Middelharnis. He was twelve years old when the war started. He emigrated to the USA in 1955 with his wife. They settled in Clifton, New Jersey, where they still live. In October of 2010 Roland published his autobiography, covering the war years and his life up to immigration to the USA. It is called 'A Boy from Flakkee'.

John Inthout
John lives in Caledonia, Michigan. He was nine years old and lived in Scheveningen when the war started.

Frans Dullemond
Frans Dullemond was born in Delft in 1936. His family arrived in Neede, in the Achterhoek region of The Netherlands in 1944. Frans came to Canada with his wife and two children in 1980, where he initially settled in Richmond, British Columbia. He now lives in Chilliwack, British Columbia.

Trix Barlage Bodde
The story of Trix's birth was written down by her mother Janny, because she was too traumatized to talk about it. Trix was born during an allied bombing raid on Rotterdam. She came to the USA in 1963 on her own, where she lived in New York City for ten years, before

moving to Connecticut. Trix translated her mother's story into English.

Carla de Boer

Carla lives in Kirkland, Washington. She lived in The Hague with her parents during the war and was fifteen years old when the Germans invaded The Netherlands.

Toni Trommelen

Toni lived in Rotterdam when the war started, she was 13 years old. In 1960 she arrived in Edmonton, Alberta with her husband and three sons, aged 7, 8 and 9. She still lives there.

John Keulen

John was born near Chicago in 1931 to Dutch immigrant parents. They returned to The Netherlands when John was two years old and settled in the Frisian village of Bakhuizen. John's parents emigrated to the United States for a second time after the war, in 1948, accompanied by John, then seventeen and his brother. John lives in Port Orange, Florida.

Liesbeth Gilbert-de Graaff

Liesbeth was born in Laren in the province of North Holland. She was five years old at the beginning of the war. When she was 17 she became a Witness of Jehovah and went to the USA to study. There she met her future husband and they married in The Netherlands. Liesbeth did missionary work in Flanders and went to the USA to live with her American husband in 1960. They lived in upstate New York until 1989, when they moved to Hampton, Virginia, where they still reside.

Ralph Schotsman

Ralph Schotsman lived in Harderwijk when the war started. He was eight years old. In 1951 he came to Canada with his parents as an eighteen year old. Initially living on a rat infested farm in Uxbridge, Ontario, the family moved to the Hamilton, Ontario area after half a year. Ralph still lives there in the house he moved into in 1960.

Freddi Bousema Weston

Freddi was born in Haarlem and was four and a half years old when the war started. She came to Canada in 1952 with her parents, Jan and Riek and her little brothers Marcel and Ludi, who were five and four years old at the time respectively. Freddi lived in Edmonton, Alberta for almost thirty years, before moving to Victoria, British Columbia, where she lives now.

Anne Hendren

Ann was twelve years old when the war started and lived in Utrecht. She now lives in Showlow, Arizona.

Caty de Graaf

Caty was born in Utrecht and turned six on the day of the German invasion in 1940. She immigrated to California in 1962 with her husband and four year old daughter. Not having completed her formal education in The Netherlands, she went to night school in the USA, now as a single mom of two, to get her high school diploma. She graduated in 1987. In 1995 she moved to Michigan to be close to her daughter and grandchildren. She still lives in Marine City in Michigan.

Enno Reckendorf
Enno lives in Hertford, North Carolina. He was ten years old when the war started.

Robert Colyn
Robert was 14 when the war started. He lived in a boarding house in Haarlem, where he went to school, while his parents had stayed behind in the Dutch East Indies where the family lived. His parents were interned in Japanese camps and he did not see them from 1939 until after the war. Robert married his high school sweetheart in 1951 and emigrated to Brazil. After four years in Brazil he took a job in Akron, Ohio, where he lived until 1962. After four years back in The Netherlands, managing a brick factory in Tricht, he moved to Salinas, California. He still lives there today.

Liesbeth Boysen-van den Blink
Liesbeth was ten years old at the start of the war.

Cecil Adema
Cecil was eleven years old at the start of the war and lived in a Speers, a very small village in the province of Friesland. He came to Canada as a single young man in 1952, because he wanted to see where those brave Canadian soldiers who liberated The Netherlands came from. It was the best thing he ever did. He married a girl from Amsterdam and they had three children together. Cecil and his wife live in Ancaster, Ontario.

Gerard van der Weyden
Gerard lived in Amsterdam when the war broke out. He was seven years old. He came to Canada in 1957

where he settled in Montreal. He is retired and lives in the greater Montreal area.

Kees Vermeer

Kees was born in The Netherlands and was almost ten years old when the Nazis invaded Holland. In 1954, he immigrated to Canada. There he went to university and graduated with a M.Sc. in Zoology from the University of British Columbia and a Ph.D. in Zoology from the University of Alberta. As a research scientist for the Government of Canada (Canadian Wildlife Service), he studied the ecology of Canadian freshwater and marine bird populations and investigated the effects of changes in sea water temperatures, chemical pollution (DDT, mercury, pentachlorophenols, dioxins and oil spills), habitat destruction (deforestation) and predation on the bird populations. He also worked in Chile and Surinam on the effects of pollutants on birds. Kees produced numerous scientific publications and was active in various professional organizations.

The Dutch in Wartime series

Book 1 - *Invasion*
Edited by Tom Bijvoet
ISBN: 978-0-9868308-0-8

Book 2 - *Under Nazi Rule*
Edited by Tom Bijvoet
ISBN: 978-0-9868308-3-9

Book 3 - *Witnessing the Holocaust*
Edited by Tom Bijvoet
ISBN: 978-0-9868308-5-3

Book 4 - *Resisting Nazi Occupation*
Edited by Anne van Arragon Hutten
ISBN: 978-0-9868308-4-6

Book 5 - *Tell your children about us*
Edited by Anne van Arragon Hutten
ISBN: 978-0-9868308-6-0

Book 6 - *War in the Indies*
Edited by Anne van Arragon Hutten
ISBN: 978-0-9868308-7-7

Book 7 - *Caught in the crossfire*
Edited by Anne van Arragon Hutten
ISBN: 978-0-9868308-8-4

Book 8 - *The Hunger Winter*
Edited by Tom Bijvoet & Anne van Arragon Hutten
ISBN: 978-0-9868308-9-1

Book 9 - *Liberation*
Edited by Anne van Arragon Hutten
ISBN: 978-0-9919981-0-4

Keep your series complete: order on-line at mokeham.com or contact Mokeham Publishing.